FIAT 500
THE AUTOBIOGRAPHY

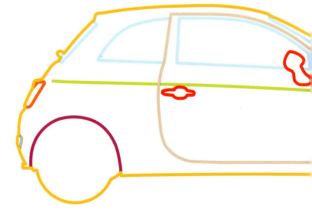

FIAT 500
THE AUTOBIOGRAPHY

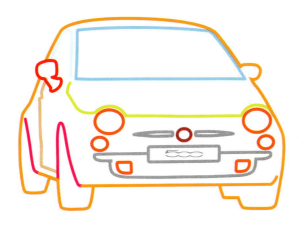

New York · Paris · London · Milan

FIAT is a registered trademark of FIAT Group Marketing & Corporate Communication SpA used under license by Chrysler Group LLC.

The images are published courtesy of Fiat and Archivio Storico Fiat.

THE PUBLISHER WOULD LIKE TO THANK THE FOLLOWING PEOPLE FOR THEIR VALUABLE CONTRIBUTIONS:
Melchiorre Drogo, Cristiana Toccafondo, Carlo Colpo, Alberto Burzio
Frida Giannini, Roberto Giolito, Ugo Nespolo, Renzo Rosso

THANKS ALSO TO:
Gioacchino Acampora, Roberto Acotto, Tiziana Bellatorre, Donatella Biffignandi, Valentina Calvello, Franco Daria, Luciana Garigliano, Andrea Peron, Alberta Simonis

Special thanks to Fiat and Archivio Storico Fiat for their contributions and cooperation for this publication and its publicity.

TEXT:
Lorenzo Ardizio

ART DIRECTION:
Sergio Pappalettera/Studio Prodesign

GRAPHIC DESIGN:
Daris Diego Del Ciello/Studio Prodesign

LAYOUT:
Gianluca Gini

EDITORIAL COORDINATION:
Giulia Dadà

PRODUCTION:
Sergio Daniotti

First published in the United States of America in 2012 by
Rizzoli International Publications, Inc.
300 Park Avenue South
New York, NY 10010
www.rizzoliusa.com

Originally published in Italian in 2011 by
RCS Libri Spa

© 2011 RCS Libri Spa, Milan

All rights reserved. No part of this publication may be reproduced, stored in a retrieval system or transmitted in any form or by any means, electronic, mechanical, photocopying, recording, or otherwise, without prior written consent of the publishers.

2012 2013 2014 2015 / 10 9 8 7 6 5 4 3 2 1

ISBN: 978-0-8478-3720-5

Library of Congress Control Number: 2011935424

Printed in Italy

THE DREAM OF OWNING A CAR	8
1. THE BIRTH	**13**
A STYLE REVOLUTION Frida Giannini	15
2. BACK TO THE FUTURE	**55**
500 WORDS ON THE 500 Ron Arad	57
THE DREAM THAT MONEY CAN BUY Ugo Nespolo	101
3. ON THE ROAD	**105**
A CINQUECENTO IN MANHATTAN Vittorio Zucconi	107

TYPICAL '50-'60 LOOK:
— FLOATING ON THE GROUND —
WITH CURVED LINES ABOVE
AND BELOW THE BODY

ITALY—HOME TO PRESTIGIOUS AUTOMOTIVE BRANDS, GREAT CHAMPIONS, TIMELESS DESIGNERS, AND STYLISTS. THE NAMES INCLUDE ALFA ROMEO, BERTONE, FARINA, FERRARI, FIAT, ITALA, LANCIA, MASERATI, NAZZARO, NUVOLARI, PININFARINA, TOURINGAUTO, VARZI, AND ZAGATO.

The universal desire for cars started to stimulate the minds, and the hearts, of politicians, industrialists, and the "masses" well before the Second World War, in a context that was far removed from what would later become known as the "economic boom," which, at least in Italy, took place in the 1950s.

As the 1930s dawned, Europeans already traveling on four wheels were yearning for motorization, and this longing was cunningly exploited by the Nazi and fascist propaganda: in Italy, and therefore at Fiat, production began on the Ballilla first, and the 500 "Topolino" later, in 1936. Concurrently, at Hitler's request, Ferdinand Porsche drew a rough sketch of the Volkswagen's "Beetle" shape, the people's car. And in France—even without the stimulus coming from a regime—the project called "Toute Petite Voiture" would be developed, which in the postwar period would become the Citroen 2CV. So it would actually be in Europe recovering from the devastation of the Second World War that all three cars would experience their golden age, later flanked by the Renault 4CV and, above all, by the Fiat Mini.

Before the war, however, 8,900 lire for the Topolino far exceeded the 5,000 lire declared by the regime as the top price for the people's car. And for the common people that car was still a distant dream. But after the war the situation changed: the success of the 500's sales exceeded all expectations and—if nothing else—overcame that era of the automobile when not just the races and the shows made the automobile poetic, but the company and the factory as well. The model plant of the Lingotto, Fiat's jewel whose praises were even sung by world-class architect Le Corbusier, soon proved to be undersized, so production had to be extended to the far less poetic warehouses of Mirafiori, triggering the overwhelming process that would lead Fiat to become a huge industry, and its native, aristocratic, and ostentatiously sober Turin—the chaotic and working-class Italian automotive capital—a catalyst that stimulated emigration and immigration between the north and south of Italy.

The dark clouds of war brought devastation, violence, and suffering. But certainly not a crisis for the large portion of the mechanical industry that would instead have to further encourage the raw automotive market of the immediate postwar period once the "golden age" of lucrative military contracts had come to an end.

That period would be short-lived. The desire to live fully, the glossy images that hailed from the other side of the Atlantic, and above all the massive aid dished out by the Marshall Plan would fuel the legendary "boom"—an economic, social, and emotional explosion within Italy that for the first time seemed capable of dreaming without the constraints of social class, profession, or age. The world of culture harnessed this positive energy, and the radio, the press, the cinema—first and foremost—and television, when it came along in 1954, gave rise to that colorful and radiant, poetic and romantic atmosphere that is universally known as "la dolce vita."

The Italian population was motorized, at least on two-wheelers: motorcycles, "lightweight motorcycles," and, most important, the overwhelming as well as inexplicable—and uniquely Italian—phenomenon, the motor scooter. The Vespa was at the front of the line. Even the automobile was no longer an unattainable dream. With great effort, by "tightening their belts," making great sacrifices, and benefiting from the invention of the providential installment plan, a 600 could be purchased and owned in just a couple years, and the family (above all, the head of the family) was content. The middle class, which was small, that had already been able to afford the Topolino could now aim high, speeding down the motorways at 110 kilometers per hour at the wheel of a very chromed 1100.

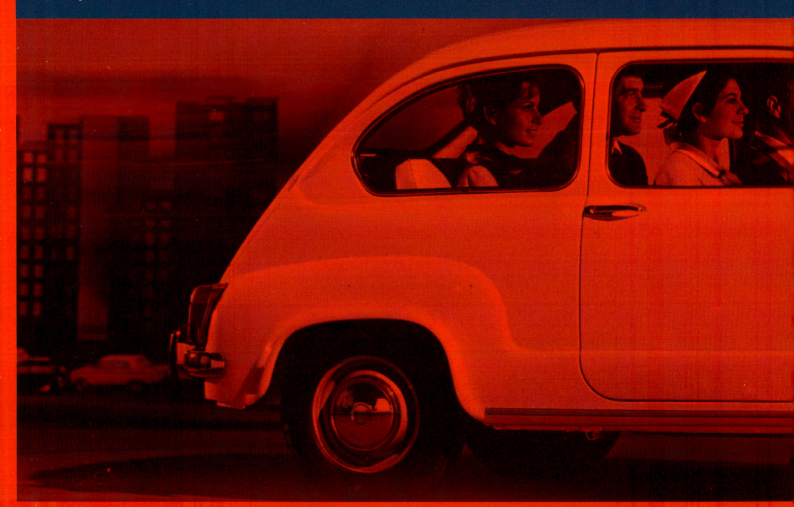

A STYLE REVOLUTION

It was born to be small, but the 500 will grow to be a big car. The manifesto of a whole generation and an icon of the "made in Italy" brand.

IN THE 1950S, THE FIAT 500 CREATED A STYLE REVOLUTION WHEN IT FIRST HIT THE ROAD.

FRIDA GIANNINI

IT QUICKLY BECAME THE MUST-HAVE CAR OF ITS TIME.

IN EUROPE, EARLY 1950S, THERE WAS A GOOD NUMBER OF WHAT WERE KNOWN AS "VETURETTES"—CYCLE CARS THAT WERE LITTLE MORE THAN A MOTORCYCLE AND MUCH LESS THAN A REAL CAR—INCLUDING ISETTA, MESSERSCHMITT, AND DORNIER DELTA.

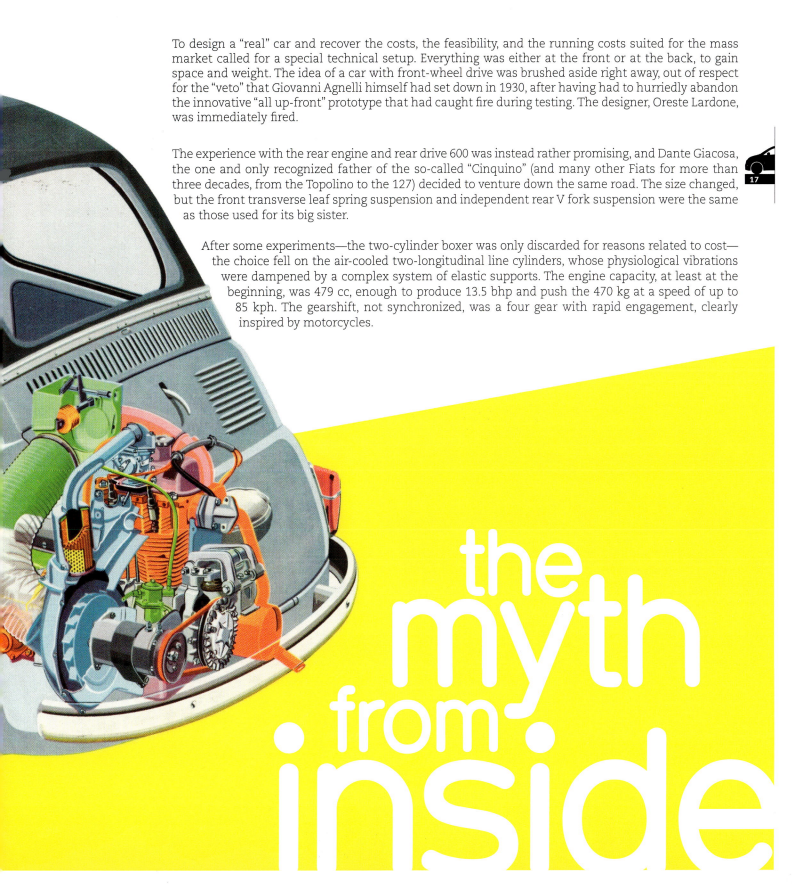

To design a "real" car and recover the costs, the feasibility, and the running costs suited for the mass market called for a special technical setup. Everything was either at the front or at the back, to gain space and weight. The idea of a car with front-wheel drive was brushed aside right away, out of respect for the "veto" that Giovanni Agnelli himself had set down in 1930, after having had to hurriedly abandon the innovative "all up-front" prototype that had caught fire during testing. The designer, Oreste Lardone, was immediately fired.

The experience with the rear engine and rear drive 600 was instead rather promising, and Dante Giacosa, the one and only recognized father of the so-called "Cinquino" (and many other Fiats for more than three decades, from the Topolino to the 127) decided to venture down the same road. The size changed, but the front transverse leaf spring suspension and independent rear V fork suspension were the same as those used for its big sister.

After some experiments—the two-cylinder boxer was only discarded for reasons related to cost—the choice fell on the air-cooled two-longitudinal line cylinders, whose physiological vibrations were dampened by a complex system of elastic supports. The engine capacity, at least at the beginning, was 479 cc, enough to produce 13.5 bhp and push the 470 kg at a speed of up to 85 kph. The gearshift, not synchronized, was a four gear with rapid engagement, clearly inspired by motorcycles.

the myth from inside

THE 500 WAS CERTAINLY NOT, AT LEAST IN DANTE GIACOSA'S EARLIEST INTENTIONS, A VEHICLE BUILT AROUND THE DRIVER. AND NOT EVEN AROUND THE ENGINE, AS WAS OFTEN THE CASE FOR UPPER-RANGE VEHICLES. IT WAS CONCEIVED STARTING RIGHT FROM THE ASSEMBLY CHAIN.

TURIN
ITALY **1961**

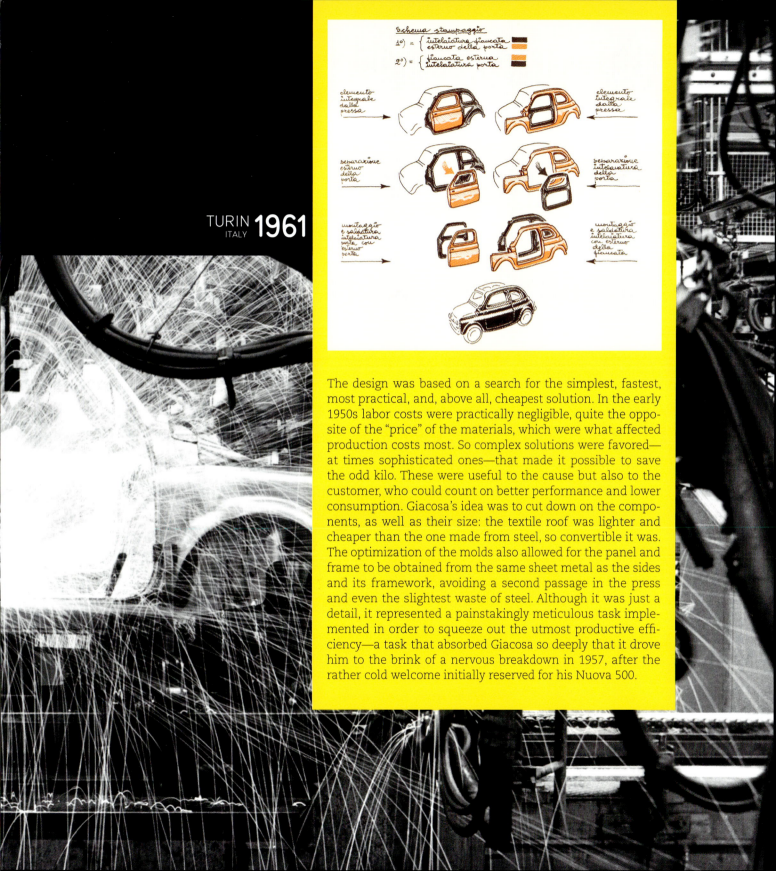

The design was based on a search for the simplest, fastest, most practical, and, above all, cheapest solution. In the early 1950s labor costs were practically negligible, quite the opposite of the "price" of the materials, which were what affected production costs most. So complex solutions were favored—at times sophisticated ones—that made it possible to save the odd kilo. These were useful to the cause but also to the customer, who could count on better performance and lower consumption. Giacosa's idea was to cut down on the components, as well as their size: the textile roof was lighter and cheaper than the one made from steel, so convertible it was. The optimization of the molds also allowed for the panel and frame to be obtained from the same sheet metal as the sides and its framework, avoiding a second passage in the press and even the slightest waste of steel. Although it was just a detail, it represented a painstakingly meticulous task implemented in order to squeeze out the utmost productive efficiency—a task that absorbed Giacosa so deeply that it drove him to the brink of a nervous breakdown in 1957, after the rather cold welcome initially reserved for his Nuova 500.

NUOVA 500

The debut vehicle was bare, austere, and "minimal," but, with its 490,000 lire price tag, not as cheap as the public had expected. No chroming, no studs on the wheels and, practically speaking, just two seats. And success was late in coming. Yet the Nuova 500 was a real car, and this fascinated, attracted, and made a whole generation dream. Fiat just needed to "adjust its aim."

NORMALE and ECONOMICA

As early as December 1957 the power rose to 15 bhp and the price dropped by 25,000 lire: the Economica version was born, flanked by the new Normale, finally equipped with vertically descending windows, padded rear seats, elegant hubcaps, and the much-desired shiny chromed profiles here and there. In addition, early buyers were refunded the price difference. The boom had begun.

SPORT

Red stripes, engine capacity increased to 499.5 cc and power to 21.5 bhp for 105 kph, along with the word "Sport" made the enthusiasts dream. But not just that: four vehicles in the first four spots in the 1958 Hockenheim 500 km paved the way to a season of great sporting achievements. Only a few of them would be sold—partly due to an extra 130,000 lire in the price—but the image-operation was a great success.

TIME LINE OF THE VERSIONS

OPEN TOP and CONVERTIBLE

At the 1959 Geneva Motor Show the "open top" made its debut. In the floor, two small "wells" were created for the feet of the rear-seat passengers, and the adoption of the last part of the roof made from metal (with a glass rear window, at last) gave it a few extra centimeters in height. Now the 500 really was a four-seater. The version with the completely cloth roof continued to be produced and was named "Trasformabile."

GIARDINIERA

The engine had to be laid on one side (which is why it was nicknamed "Sole," as in "fish") to hide it under the loading floor, and thus created the station wagon version of the 500, or rather the so-called "Giardiniera." So much space on board, loading room, convenience, and versatility—even a little extra power. The Giardiniera would become a legend.

500 D

The year of the definitive consecration was 1960. The engine size of the Nuova 500 D rose to 499.5 cc and the power to 18 bhp. The list price also went up by 15,000 lire, but this was a price that customers were happy to pay if it meant having what had at last become the much-longed-for utility car. Just improvements but—as we all know—it's the details that always make the difference.

500 F

In 1965 the new norms dictated that doors had to be hinged "frontward," and Fiat took this opportunity to spruce up the whole vehicle: the 500 F was born. Tastes changed too and all those shiny profiles, so much in demand just ten years earlier, were removed, in favor of elegance. The 500 F would become the best-selling family car by far.

500 L

L stands for "luxury." And the version of the 500 "with tubes" saw the light of day in 1968. Clearly in view were the tubular reinforcements of the bumpers, and these came with a shiny profile here and there. Features inside the car included folding seats, trays and containers for objects, and, above all, a dashboard finished with black vinyl, on which the speedometer of the Fiat 850 stood out with a scale that went all the way up to 130 kph.

500 R

The last-born; it was 1972. The range already included the 126, but the 500 still had its admirers. No more chrome, a lozenge-shaped official badge on the grille, refined but simplified interiors, and, under the hood, the 594 bhp engine of the 126, but depowered to 18 bhp. At last a top speed of 100 kph could be reached and the vehicle as a whole was mature and reliable. But the times... they were a-changin'.

ABARTH

Pages have been written, along with books, on the special relationship that linked the 500 with the name Abarth. It may have been the sports results, the far-sightedness of Carlo Abarth in interpreting and envisioning the desires of the customers, or the automobile designer's "professional" approach. In any case, the 500s with the scorpion on the grille even today emerge powerfully from the deep sea of cars prepared by more or less well-known brands, by specialized auto body shops, or, at times, in the garages in the street below to "touch 100 km."

The first 500 Abarth was presented in 1957, but its success was nothing to write home about; the same could be said for the standard version. A second series, the following year, received better results, this time thanks to the competition of the 500 Sport. Then came the days of the race against the record books and, first with a vehicle "close" to the one produced in series and later with a single-seater with Pinin Farina bodywork (it wouldn't be called a Pininfarina until the following year), twenty-one records would be broken.

The turnaround took place with the 595 in 1963: in the toolbox—today's assembly kit—for conversion supplied by Abarth, you could find everything you needed, screws and straps included. But above all a new cylinder block, the 595 cc, capable of taking the power up to 27 bhp, for 121 kph. Another 5 bhp would be added to the SS version and the subsequent 695, with increased engine capacity. In 1964 there would be a 38 bhp SS version for the 695 as well, with a top speed of 140 kph, for which a "racing setup" would be launched the following year. Victories, records, podium finishes. But above all, the dreams and longings of a whole generation of young race drivers or sports enthusiasts. The appeal—and the performances—of the 500 Abarth did not fail to interest the state police force as well, which would purchase some for the anti–bag-snatching police patrols. And even Fiat itself, which in 1971 would take over the ownership of the brand of the scorpion, leaving Carlo Abarth "with his pockets full of money, but no longer the boss in his own home."

SPECIALS

IT WAS STILL THE ERA OF THE CUSTOM-BUILT CAR, THE "SPECIALS" DRESSED UP BY THE BEST-KNOWN ITALIAN BODY-MAKERS—OR BY SOME "OUTSIDER." AND THE 500, WITH ITS YOUTHFUL, CAREFREE, FRESH PLEASANTNESS, WAS AN IDEAL STARTING POINT. BUT IT WAS ALSO THE ERA OF SPECIALLY PREPARED VERSIONS AND ELABORATIONS, WHETHER SPORTY OR NOT.

GIANNINI

The only brand capable of competing with Abarth, in terms of performance, commercial success, and sports results, would be the Roman car manufacturer Giannini. The war horses would be the 25 bhp 500 TV, the 590 GT, with a engine capacity of 586 cc, 35 bhp, and 120 kph, and the respective further-enhanced Special versions. The 350 Economica, featuring reduced bhp but capable of offering adequate performance, would also be put on the market—a wink at the German market, where it could still be driven with the still widespread license for small cars. Instead, the project for a 700 bhp with a four-cylinder boxer engine had no follow-up.

500 ABARTH ZAGATO
A tough and thoroughbred racing car that drew its inspiration from the better-known—and more powerful—GT with the Z on the side, the 500 Abarth Zagato would make its presence felt in racing too, winning the Italian title in 1958 with Ovidio Capelli at the wheel.

FRUA
Chromed profiles, shiny wheel bases. But also the profile of a boat, its "maritime" bearing emphasized by the sunken headlights and the frameless windshield.

500 ABARTH COUPÉ PININFARINA
Presented in Turin in 1957, its engine was revamped by Abarth—but it would never be produced.

MAGGIOLINA FRANCIS LOMBARDI
The body-makers in Vercelli, Piedmont, also suggested a nice convertible that didn't even try to hide the fact—starting with the name itself—that it was directly inspired by the Volkswagen Beetle. This car would not be mass-produced.

JOLLY GHIA
Proposed by Ghia, the Jolly would be one of the greatest successes for the "limited editions": it was a typical "beach buggy," with no roof or doors. The seats made of wicker were ideal for people wearing bathing suits, and the line made it likeable and youthful. Several versions were made and there were also VIP clients.

GAMINE VIGNALE
In French *gamine* means "mischievous." In fact, Vignale's would be a car with an old-fashioned appearance that would have huge commercial success, above all in the French market.

SAVIO
Another "miniature" spider made in a very short time—and with some uncertainty—for the Turin Motor Show. The long hood, a nod to grand touring, was meant to hide the rear engine.

A QUESTION OF STYLE

Italians simply adore chrome: they see it as the yardstick for measuring luxury, wealth, and beauty. Nor do they disdain tail fins and bumpers, American-style solutions that they could admire right alongside the pictures of movie stars, sighing as they leafed through glossy magazines.

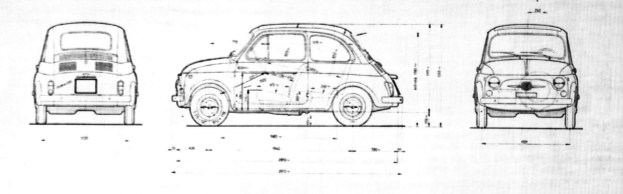

A "minimalist" car, at least according to Giacosa, could—actually had to—be another thing altogether: "Italians longed to have a car, and they would have been content with a small space, as long as it had four wheels; however small, a car was always going to be more comfortable than a motor scooter, especially in winter and on rainy days."

The inspiration for the first project could only be the motor scooter. Actually, the scooter par excellence, i.e., the Vespa. The outline was sketched out, and while the front was that of a car, complete with a grille, the rest of the bodywork drew its inspiration instead from the two-wheeler, especially in the rear, where the wheel boxes were streamlined almost like a Vespa's. Plus, it had a roof, but no doors, which could be replaced in an emergency by two cloth covers. Also, the engine, a two-cylinder two-stroke 200 cc, couldn't really be considered something a car would normally have.

A second project drew inspiration from the drawings sent to Turin by Franz Bauhof, a technician at Deutsche Fiat in Heilbronn. The rear engine was still a motorcycle ILO, but in the design many features of what would become the Nuova 500 were already visible. After a few months, in the fall of 1953, Mirafiori also received a prototype from Germany. Giacosa welcomed the new crisp lines, which abandoned once and for all any hint of a fender, as it was based, on the contrary, on two overlapping volumes.

But every possibility had to be examined, and in the following spring, the President's Board was given two ideas for a new car: the first one copied the lines of the 600 but in miniature, while the second one, called 110-518, was already the newborn 500. Giacosa fought hard for a more modern solution. The management—albeit with some doubts—gave the go-ahead. The hard work of optimization began, which characterized the vehicle's gestation period: nothing was left to chance and the decision was made to lower the roof of the tail in order to make the two rear seats less comfortable—thus averting the danger of "cannibalizing" the 600's market.

Savings were made on everything: room, comfort, optionals, finishing—following Henry Ford's philosophy that "all you need is a car to feel rich." But Italian drivers, even those not yet born, were already very demanding.

When the 500 saw the light of day with the parade of beauty queens in July 1957, the cinema era of *La Dolce Vita* had come to an end—an era of Vespas, Lambrettas, a few Topolinos, and a great deal of chrome clearly inspired by the North American market. And tail fins, eight-cylinder engines, and dimensions on this side of the ocean were usually seen in trucks. These were the years when movie actors and actresses became stars, when Sofia Villani Scicolone became Sophia Loren, and when, after years of austere neorealism, the images of ruins and furrowed faces of farmers started to disappear from the movies to make way for plots and screenplays that would turn Italy into the stuff of fairy tales, dreams, and love stories.

LA DOLCE VITA

TURIN
ITALY 1957

But in the cities, apartments were still being built that would be bought with thirty-year mortgages; the same apartment blocks that today we would like to see vanish from the historic centers, that were, until a few years ago, the absolute protagonists of a thousand-year-old landscape. In the countryside, the earth was tilled in the sun, and in the factories men and women broke their backs for 30,000 lire a month. Far from the papier-mâché of the Cinecittà film studios, la dolce vita had yet to come . . . at least not until July 4, 1957.

THEY CHALLENGE BIASES, MORE OFTEN SARCASM, AND WOMEN AT LAST CAN SIT AT THE WHEEL. IT IS THE CHANCE TO GO TO WORK, TO GO SHOPPING, TO GO SEE FRIENDS. AT TIMES IN SECRET. FREELY.

"I would say that it really is made for women because we not only thought hard about their tastes, but also how they might use it in the city. By this I don't mean that women are not good drivers, quite the opposite, but that a certain laziness in changing gears is rather common." That was Dante Giacosa again, in the interview he gave on the radio on July 2, 1957, on the eve of the great parade for the launch of the 500. The question obviously was this: "So is it especially suited to women?"

Even today this is a recurring question: can a new car satisfy women's taste in any particular way? But in 1957 the meaning was very different. The car was the family car, driven by the head of the family. And when the rear seats—if there were any—were empty, at the steering wheel sat a bachelor. The car had undoubted charm. In any case, women rarely left the passenger seat.

Another pattern smashed by the 500, another piece of an era that collapsed in the face of modernity. The year 1968 had nothing to do with it. Actually 1968 was one of the effects of a changing world: women's liberation, independence, freedom, individual expression. Far from the banners of the feminist movement, these were the trends that the market had already envisaged. On advertising posters, there were still families and bachelors. But also a lot of women, single women, appealing, open-minded, and with about a thousand expressions on their faces.

The 500—also but not only in its special versions—pulled at the heartstrings of the era's most famous people. Juan Manuel Fangio, Yul Brynner, Aristotle Onassis, Pope Paul VI, Jayne Mansfield, Alberto Sordi, and Lyndon Johnson are just a few of the characters who stopped in front of the camera lens as they stood beside a Fiat 500. But many more of them had one in their garage, used it to move quickly through the traffic, for work or just for pure pleasure. The first and foremost was the president of the Italian Republic Sandro Pertini. That was the sheer charm of the 500: freedom and independence. And no one could fail to succumb to it.

DARLING OF THE CELEBRITIES

GREETINGS FROM ITALY

VENICE
ITALY **1960**

THE 600 MAY WELL HAVE MOTORIZED ITALIANS, BUT THE 500 SET THEM FREE.

The 500 was clearly the mirror of 1950s and 1960s Italy. A time of upheavals, revolutions, and major changes in society. The car made to motorize the working class broke the patterns and became as transversal as it was impossible to classify. Journalists often say today that "you could never know if the owner was a student, his teacher, a worker, or a wealthy gentleman who had left his big sedan in the garage so that he could travel around completely free. . . ." And this was indeed the ways things stood.

If the Fiat managers' and the Fiat engineers' idea—their goal—was to motorize Italy with the 500, then it is apparent that a good deal of the task had already been performed by its big sister. It was with the 600 that for the first time the office workers went to work by car and took their families to the beach in the summer. Caravans of fathers in ostentatiously tie-less shirts, excitable wives seated beside them, and children with their hands hanging outside the windows, half-submerged by heaps of luggage—all of them in long lines headed toward the "holiday resorts," from August 1 to 31.

WELCOME, BAMBINA!

New Zealand assembled just more than five thousand Fiat 500s, making it the first real vehicle for the masses. It's a story that repeated itself. And the little blessed event was christened "Bambina," written just like that, in Italian. In 1964, one was even sent to the scientists stationed at Scott Base, in the Antarctic, to be used as a shuttle with the United States station at McMurdo Sound.

The 500 spread modestly all around the world, at times modified to satisfy the different tastes; in India they had two-color bodies, in the United States larger headlights were required, in Germany a chromed drain on the roof was added, and in hot countries the roof was made from white cloth instead of black.

Some versions, with a few changes, were then produced on license; the most famous were the Nsu Fiat from Heilbronn-am-Neckar, which differed for their body, the work of Weinsberg, and the Austrians of Steyr-Puch, in this case equipped with a powerful two-cylinder boxer. Highly sought-after by racers, also Italians, it was soon "outlawed" by the race regulations of the Bel Paese.

But the "Cinquino" would often be pictured as it made its way through the African jungle or as it rode through English towns. Or perhaps at the airport, about to venture off. Where to? Who knows?

THE 500 DEPARTING ON AN ALITALIA CARGO PLANE FOR THE 1958 COURSE DE LA COTE. ITS DESTINATIONS WILL INCLUDE TAHITI, NEW ZEALAND, HOLLAND, AND TANGIERS.

THE "CINQUINO" EASILY ADAPTED TO ALL DIFFERENT CLIMATES. FROM EQUATORIAL AFRICA TO THE ANTARCTIC, WHERE IT WOULD BE USED AS A SERVICE CAR AT THE SCOTT BASE.

POSTERS OF AN ERA

THERE WAS A TIME—A VERY COLORFUL AND FASCINATING ONE—WHEN THE HISTORY OF THE CAR COULD BE TOLD THROUGH THE ADVERTISING POSTERS, THE SO-CALLED AFFICHE.

Then came television, and the way of "communicating" the car changed. The story of the 500 was told by a number of photographers, graphic designers, and draftsmen: at first it was the first family car; then simply the first car.

The car can be the star of a film, and often that has been the case. The Lancia Aurelia B24 of *Il sorpasso (The Easy Life)* wrote a page in the history of Italian cinema, just as the Alfa Romeo "Duetto" in *The Graduate* wrote a chapter in Hollywood history.

The 500 became more than an Italian star. It became a part of Italy—part of the landscape, the plots, the imagery, the backdrop. Today there is no film—whether Italian or foreign—set in the Bel Paese in which at least once, even if only by chance, a 500 is not noticed. Paris is recognized by its Eiffel Tower, London by Big Ben. For Italy, even just a 500 standing at a red light is enough.

The wait for the launch of the 500 was spasmodic. Everyone, without exception, awaited the fateful day, as one would await the results of high school exams: pass or fail. And the opinion on the car would be of the same sort: it would be a dream come true or the umpteenth illusion of radical change. The newspaper headlines mirrored this widespread feeling. It was enough to flood generations of drivers—or people just waiting to become drivers—with optimism.

LA NUOVA 500

Ai primi di luglio la Fiat presenterà questa piccola vettura, che non è una motocicletta coperta ma veramente una automobile, la quale grazie alla vendita a lunga rateizzazione sarà la prima vettura di tanti che da tempo sognavano una macchina.

La nostra presentazione è appena una anticipazione, con dati e fotografie non fornite dalla Casa; naturalmente faremo presto una esauriente completa prova con le illustrazioni di tutti i particolari.

E' confermato che per il Salone di Torino verrà presentata l'edizione di lusso «la "Bianchina"» costruita negli stabilimenti di Desio.

500 WORDS ON THE 500

The 500 reinvents itself so that it will always be the right car at the right time. Fifty years have gone by, but its charm hasn't changed at all.

SOME THIRTY YEARS AGO I WENT TO ROME AND WAS AMAZED BY THE NUMBER OF 500S ON THE STREETS. IT'S FUNNY, YOU COULD HARDLY SPOT A 600, AND IT MADE YOU WONDER WHY.

RON ARAD

THE 600 WAS SLIGHTLY BIGGER, IT HAD FOUR CYLINDERS, THERE WAS MORE "CAR" IN IT, AND YET IT DIDN'T SURVIVE LIKE THE 500 DID.

The conclusion I came to was that the 500 proved that refusing to make compromises pays off. If you want to make a small car—the smallest car—then make it small. I believe in extremes, and when extremes work, they work well.

In Rome, I decided that I wanted one in London, and indeed, on the way home from the Heathrow Airport, at a red traffic light, I saw someone driving a Fiat 500. I rolled down my car window and asked the driver, "Are you selling?" He said, "Yes." I asked, "How much?" He said, "Five hundred," and I said, "What's your address?" The address he gave me was very near my house. A few hours later the car was mine.

That's when I started my relationship with the Proetti family. They are an Italian family living in London with a small garage dedicated to Cinquecentos. Delightful. I thought it meant that this car would never die. It was very useful for the school-runs in the morning, and my daughters felt very special being driven in the little Fiat 500 (we even made a song about it) as opposed to all their friends who were driven in 4 x 4 monsters. A few years later, two of my students at the Royal College of Art, Arash and Eddie, told me that they wanted to paint a car glow-in-the-dark. It was obvious to me that it should be the 500. Now the rust is winning over the glow-in-the-dark paint.

The car is not going anywhere. It knows it is soon going to become a piece of art. I'm waiting for moss to take over the rust and then we'll see.

Before the launch of the new 500 I was approached by Fiat to create an homage to the old 500, and I came up with Fiat 5000000, a extra-long wooden crate with two identical vintage Fiat 500s poking out of each end—one side showing the front of the car, the other side showing the tail, like a stretched Fiat 500. The front number plate read "ROMA," and the back "АМОЯ." Later, I was asked to personalize a new Fiat 500. It was obvious to me that its ancestors should be referred to. I thought it would be nice to have a line drawing of the original Fiat 500 printed on the side of the new one, sharing the center of the rear wheels. When I presented it to Fiat they were initially taken aback, asking, "Can we stretch the old 500? . . . We feel a little embarrassed." I said, "No, of course you can't stretch it." "Can we put it in the center?" "No, they must share the rear wheels—don't be embarrassed—you made a great car. Yes it's bigger, yes it's more powerful. I know it's not the old Cinquecento, but we can't re-create or reconstruct the past, nor do we need to. Well done, we love the new Fiat 500."

Ron Arad

AMAZING PAST

BETTER FUTURE

The launch of the "new" 500 in 2007 was quite a shock—the same level of excitement that had been anticipated by the Trepiuno concept three years earlier. And the vaguely melancholic expression "nostalgia effect" kept popping up. Perhaps reference was being made to the car's retro design, promoted by the marketing strategy that aimed at those for whom the 500, in its 1957 version, represented a piece of a life lived, of one's own past, of one's own memories. Whatever the case may be, it's worth digging deep inside that design, inside the contents, inside the reasons—or the emotions—of those who wanted to have a new "Cinquino" in the garage in order to understand that this time it had absolutely nothing to do with a simple trip down memory lane.

Today, as then, the 500 is appealing for its youthful likability—a somewhat carefree, but still trustworthy automobile whose contents and worldly and trendy vocations are so much a part of it. And once again the admiring gazes come from all directions, transcending social background, economic purchasing power, gender—for sure—and also the potential purchasers' age range.

"TODAY, AS THEN,
THE 500 IS APPEALING FOR
ITS YOUTHFUL LIKABILITY."

Only a brave manufacturer would bring out the same advertising images half a century after they were first introduced. The same characters, the same settings, and the same moods were featured. In the case of the 500, however, the bond between the "old" and the "new" went a lot deeper: it was a bond that allowed the company to touch the same heartstrings in order to move and amaze the public.

Perhaps something had changed: in 1957, and even more so in the years that followed, except for the car's particular appeal for those who were and are still avid "collectors" the 500 almost unexpectedly emerged as a transversal vehicle: a city car, practical but also a little chic. In 2007 this became instead the very aim of the manufacturer, pursued with care and determination from the moment the first line was traced out on paper.

"THE 500 ALMOST UNEXPECTEDLY EMERGED AS A TRANSVERSAL VEHICLE: A CITY CAR, PRACTICAL BUT ALSO A LITTLE CHIC."

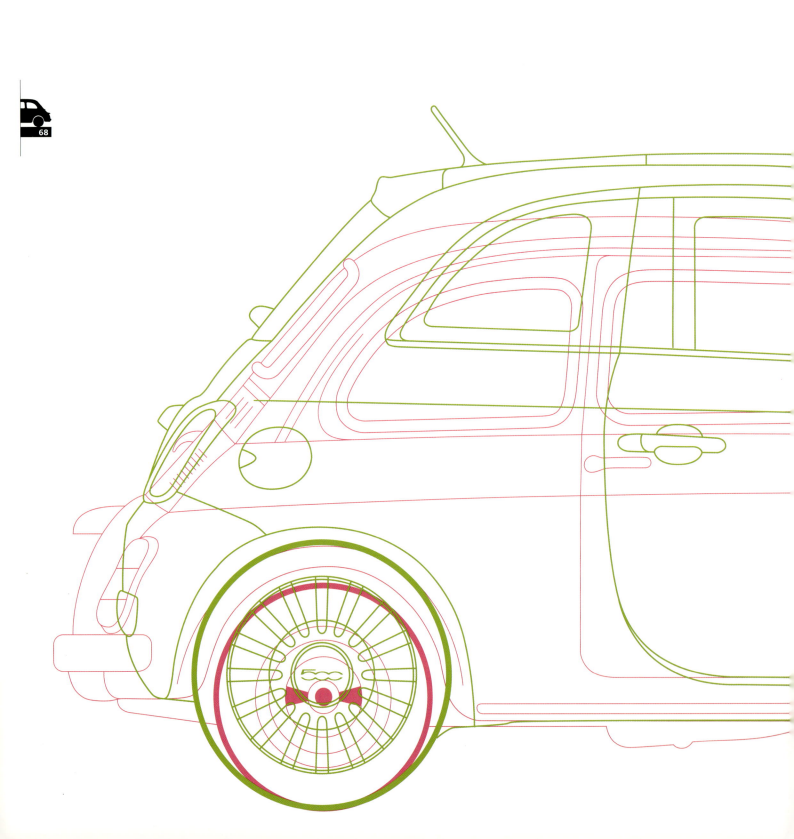

500 OUT OF 500. THE SIZE CHANGED,

as did the proportions. The mechanics, the performance, and the price—all changed. There were no elements—not a single line—in common between the 500 made in 1957 (the legendary one) and the 500 of fifty years later. And yet looking at each one of them individually, first one and then the other, we discover that they really were the same car—with the same friendliness, the same smile, the same distinct appeal, an expression of the same yearning for freedom and independence. It wasn't the folds in the metal that were copied, but the spirit.

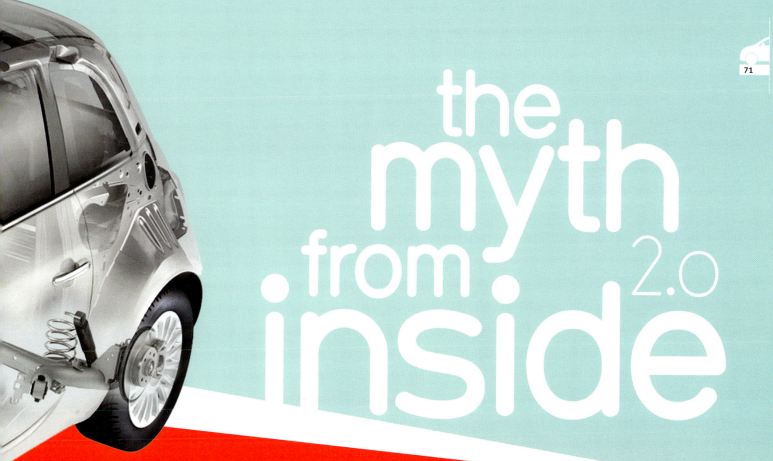

the myth from inside 2.0

Once again the designers were tangling with a city car. More important than the fact that the new 500 was heir to the legendary 500 was the intention that this was a real city car for the twenty-first century.

If Giacosa's obsession had been to save weight and steel for his child, the priorities, fifty years later, were different and much more numerous. Safety, room, consumption, comfort, emissions, aerodynamics, and maintenance of the original design—just some of the features that made the new model's "production costs" drop down the charts, and by a number of places at that.

First of all, it was necessary to find the "synergies" inside or outside the group, that is, the use of parts, platforms, and production lines common to other models that could better cushion the plant's design and equipment costs. After the idea of using a shorter version of the Punto's platform was tossed around, the choice fell on the Panda's, which was lighter and more modern. The technology was also very much appreciated by Ford, which decided to also produce, on the same basis and on the same production lines in Tychy, Poland, the "new" Ka.

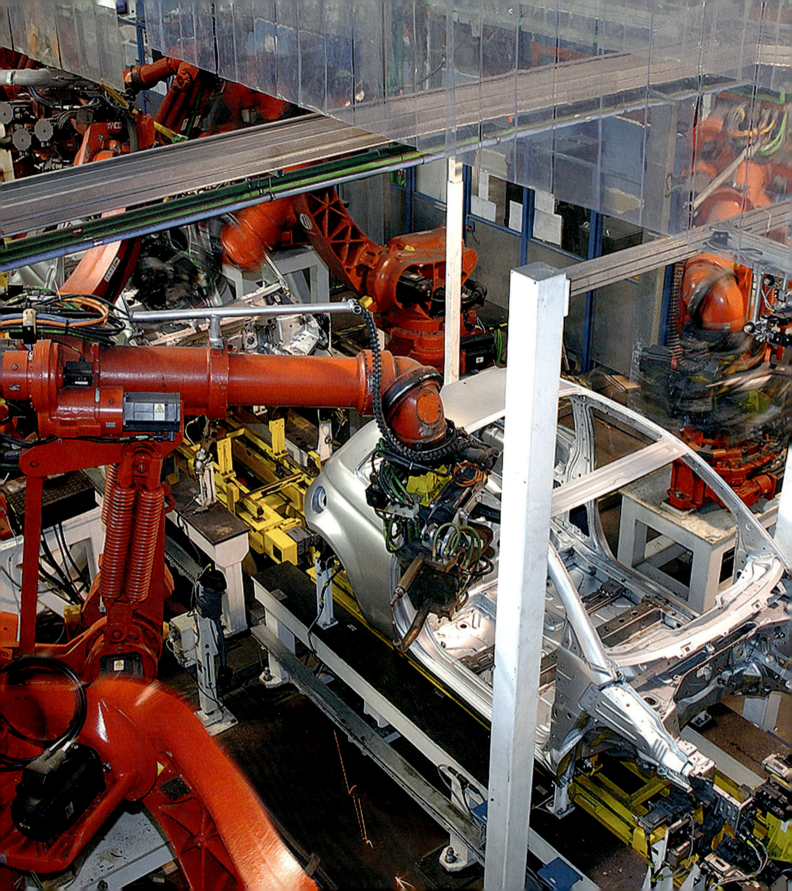

The old taboo of front-wheel drive had for some years been smashed, so the new 500 was an "all up front" with a McPherson front axle and a torque rear axle, according to a universally consolidated model for this kind of car. This assured reliability, safety, and solid and gratifying road handling.

In 2007 even the choice of engines were spread over several possibilities, to satisfy the tastes—and the need for mobility—of every customer: the entry level was a 1.2 cc, 69 bhp gas-driven engine, flanked by a snappier 1.4 that instead featured 100 bhp. In the meantime in Europe the "bomb" of modern common rail turbo diesels had exploded and, thanks to this technology inaugurated by Fiat, in just a few years, diesel engines abandoned the vans and large sedans to be fitted in high-range cars, sports cars, and even convertibles. The 500 did not miss out on this, and was put on the market with the lively 1.3 Multijet with 75 bhp; over the following years its power would be increased to 95 bhp.

The cars in the presentation were all four-cylinder engines as the market had already for some time excluded—somewhat snobbishly—that glorious two-cylinder family with which the 500 had conquered the world. But the times were a-changin' and, in the name of the trend that's universally known as "downsizing," in the technical offices of the various manufacturers, engines with two or three cylinders were reappearing. Above all, in the Fiat design offices (now joined under the initials FPT, Fiat Powertrain Technologies), a great deal of attention was given to the development of the small TwinAir, aspirated or turbo, which debuted with the 500 in 2011.

TYCHY
POLAND **2007**

500

The "original" version, available from the very beginning in Italy with three engine types—two gas and one diesel—and three looks to choose from—Pop, Lounge, and Sport—besides a virtually endless range of personalization. Practical, small, lively, and extremely attractive, it rediscovered, but without copying, the design of the old "Cinquino." It was love at first sight.

TIME LINE OF THE VERSIONS

500C

The fascination with "open cars" showed no signs of ever dying out. So how could there not be a version dedicated to the lovers of driving in open air, as they say. This car was presented in 2009, after a lot of rumors concerning the type of roof. With or without a folding frame? In textile or metal? In the end it would come with both a folding frame and textile: certainly not for the sake of saving money, but for beauty.

ABARTH 500

After years of "mufflers" and remakes, Abarth became famous, thanks to the successes of "its very own" 500s—so much so that Fiat would take over the brand. A brand that today identifies the meanest of the versions: the front was lengthened to accommodate the turbo, the real reason for the 130 bhp produced by the 1.4. Then it got lower, wider, and the whole car was reinterpreted. The charm was intense, like a Scorpion's—and so was the performance.

ABARTH 500C

It might well be "poetic license" because an automobile designer—and Carlo Abarth was one of the best—would never refit a convertible: it just wouldn't be racetrack material. But the Abarth 500C was a success. For some it was the open version of the Abarth, for others it was the C that stood for "*cattiva*" ("a mean machine"), but no one could resist its seduction.

ABARTH 500 ESSEESSE

The assembly kit came in a wooden box, just like in the old days: suspensions, brakes, engine, and, above all, the exhaust. The performance on this racy version of the Abarth was absolutely breathtaking: 160 bhp and well above 210 kph. But for the more demanding this could go even higher up with the special versions; up to the almost 200 bhp of the Trofeos that raced on the track.

TWINAIR

Don't call it an entry-level car! At last, in 2011, the two-cylinder was back. It was the smallest one in the family, but also the one that sparkled the most. Even the debut version aimed at sportiness. The small 0.9 liter, with MultiAir technology, was at first presented in an 85 bhp turbo version. But we all know that this was just the beginning.

GUCCI

A symbol of "Made in Italy," the 500 could not be better matched—the correct term—than with another iconic name: Gucci. Frida Giannini, creative director of the prestigious fashion house, worked closely with Centro Stile Fiat, and the result, a very fashionable car both inside and out, was an immediate success.

500 COUPÉ ZAGATO

The Milanese firm had already signed a version of the "old" 500. So on view at the Geneva Motor Show in 2011 was an interpretation of the new one: the line of a coupé, aggressive appearance, details that foreshadowed the future models, and those two humps on the roof that over the years have often identified the "specials" with the Z on the side.

SPECIALS

TODAY, JUST LIKE BEFORE, AN ICON SUCH AS THE 500 KNOWS HOW TO ATTRACT THE STYLISTS, THE ENGINEERS, AND THE ENTHUSIASTS—LEAVING FREEDOM, FOR ONCE, TO THE FLAIR OF THE DESIGNERS.

DA 0 A 100

On the French market it had been christened—with some variants—Abarth Speedgray Neubauer. In any case, a total of 100 "specials" based on the "Esseeesse" were made, dedicated to the records achieved by the "old" 500 Monza. They were painted Nuvolari Gray but featured the exclusive "Monza" muffler.

500 BY DIESEL
Limited Edition

It was born as a limited edition, but also ended up in the price lists. The binomial car fashion relived in this determined and highly personal 500, subsequently also available in the C version. It came in Green, Bronze by Diesel, and Midnight Indigo. And the many exclusive details made the difference. On all of the engines.

BICOLORE

Two colors for the "old" 500, at least in Italy, had never even been suggested. But now this paint job was experiencing its golden moment with the 500; with its lighthearted and sort of old-fashioned line, it cut a fine figure for itself. And the two colors of the body could also be seen in the interiors.

OPENING EDITION

These were the first five hundred 500s previewed. They were displayed in their "Opening" and "Cappellini" editions, with the unmistakable blue livery, which had first appeared at the Cappellini stand for the 2007 Milan Furniture Fair. Even Abarth would have its Opening Edition series, all five hundred of them, complete with the Esseeesse kit.

500 MONZA ROMEO FERRARIS

The automobile designer Romeo Ferraris went back to the 500 Abarth and took it to the extreme, at least with regard to the road versions. White with red and blue stripes (the colors of the Monza racetrack), its suspensions and brakes were completely overhauled, but above all the 1.4-liter turbo was increased to 260 bhp.

695 TRIBUTO FERRARI

It derived from the 500 Abarth. And with this name it could not have been otherwise. But, in the name of the brand to which it was dedicated, Ferrari, it underwent a massive injection of technology. Starting from the power: 180 bhp for 225 kph.

TENDER TWO CASTAGNA

It was the return of the beach buggies, again thanks to Castagna. Four different interpretations for every taste, with accessories, precious materials, wood, and, above all, charm—in abundance. For the more demanding there was a fridge for the champagne and a portable shower for after the beach.

500 MILLESIMA

The first half a million 500s produced deserved a celebration. No books, events, or major endorsements, only a body covered by 1,500 photographs of famous or not so famous people, or just plain enthusiasts who wanted—by using a dedicated Web site—to "put their face" on the 500.

500 BARBIE

Barbie was fifty years old and Mattel couldn't help thinking about the 500. From its request to Fiat came a shockingly pink 500. Shocking pink. "Something" of the kind would even end up being produced: the 500 So Pink.

THE 500 IS THE CAR THAT SYMBOLIZES ITALY, AND ITS RESTYLING HAS TURNED IT INTO THE COOLEST, SEXIEST CAR FOR YOUNG PEOPLE TODAY. THIS IS WHY DIESEL WAS HAPPY TO WORK WITH FIAT ON THE FIRST SPECIAL EDITION OF THE 500. TRULY AN ICON OF STYLE THAT SUMS UP ALL THE FEATURES THAT HAVE MADE OUR BRAND SO POPULAR ACROSS THE WORLD. Renzo Rosso

TRAVELING IN STYLE HAS ALSO BEEN AT THE HEART OF GUCCI EVER SINCE GUCCIO GUCCI FOUNDED HIS COMPANY AS A PRODUCER OF LEATHER TRUNKS, SUITCASES, AND HANDBAGS IN 1921. SO, WHEN LAPO ELKANN SUGGESTED THE IDEA OF THIS COLLABORATION, IT STRUCK ME AS A PERFECT OPPORTUNITY TO CREATE A NEW MODERN TRAVEL STATEMENT IN GUCCI'S NINETIETH ANNIVERSARY YEAR.

Frida Giannini

The main idea was to build a compact, functional, and attractive car: the state of the art in its segment. Fiat had the technology, the resources, and the experience to do it. The second step was to "invent" a style capable of attracting and satisfying the market, which was becoming increasingly careful and demanding.

That was when the desire—it had never completely died out—to remake the 500 was rediscovered. A car that had been a Fiat icon and, in its day and age, meant even more for Italians.

Combining the two factors was certainly not an easy task: very often style and functionality don't move at the same pace. But in the case of the 500, such was the aim, the inspiration, and the determination of the team at the Centro Stile Fiat, led then, as now, by Roberto Giolito, to move to production without delay. Sometimes you need several teams—outside teams, too—and dozens of drafts to be able to finally settle on the right model. In this case only three proposals were needed to capture the spirit of the 500 of the olden days and to combine it with the best technology available.

First was the Trepiuno concept and soon afterward—with hardly any changes at all—the new 500 was born: a winning design, spontaneous and instantly recognizable. The "Cinquino" of the third millennium could not have been any other way.

STAR DESIGN

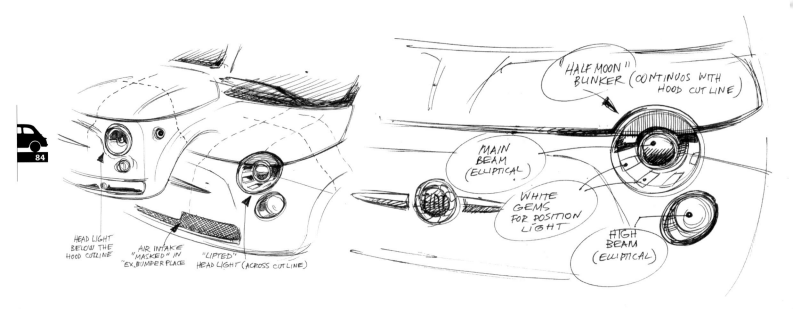

Roberto Giolito

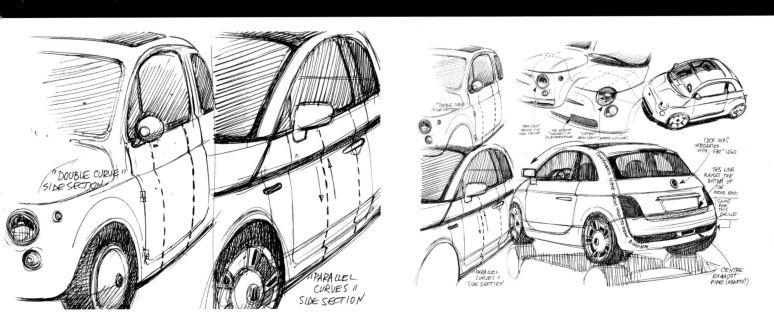

In my career as a designer, time and time again I've seen car builders and freelance designers present Fiat with different interpretations of the so-called 500 "theme." Usually this has entailed a formal exercise of transposing some of the features belonging to the original 500 into a more modern language, and in any case one that can be implemented. The operation that Fiat has carried out with the contemporary Fiat instead starts out from an analysis of how to reinvent a small car that, without extravagance or big revolutions in technology, will eventually define a new type of product focused on the goal, one that will gratify the customer with its carefully planned design and convince him or her with its proportions.

ABOVE ALL THE 500 IS A PRODUCT THAT HAS ALL THE FEATURES OF USABILITY THAT YOU'D EXPECT FROM A CAR LIKE THIS, FEATURES LIKE SAFETY, THE VERSATILITY OF ITS MECHANICS AND OPTIONALS, RUNNING COSTS AND LOW EMISSION, WHICH WOULD LEAD US TO SAY THAT TODAY'S 500 IS SIMPLY THE CAR THAT WE FELT LIKE MAKING AT FIAT TODAY.

Roberto Giolito

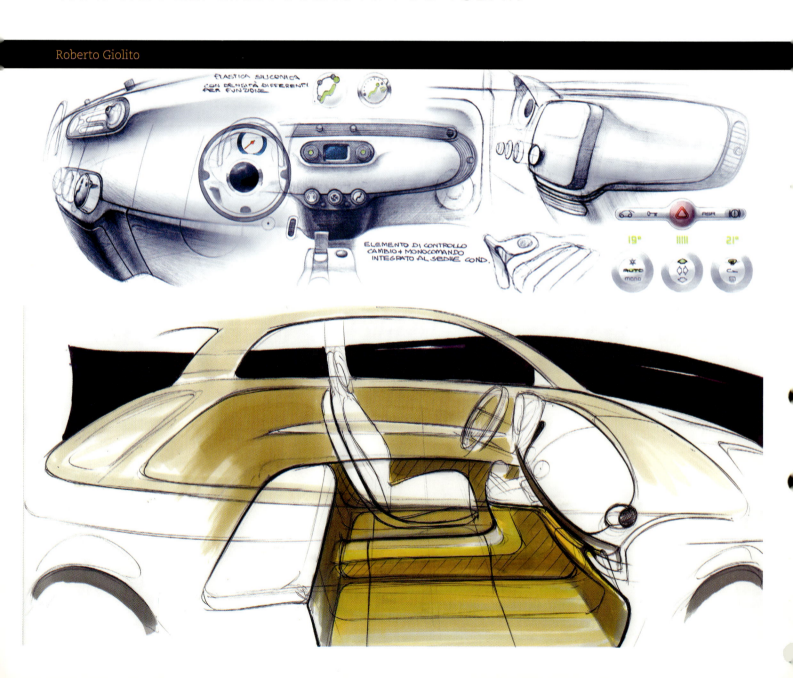

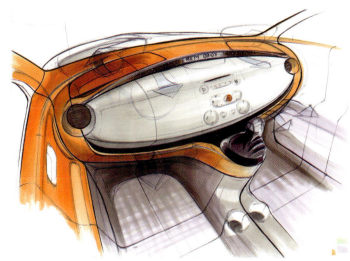
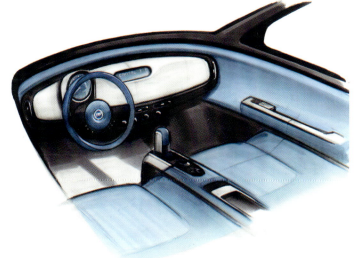

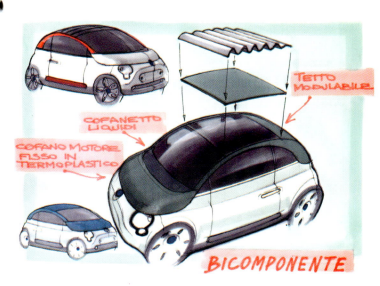

TETTO MODULABILE
COFANETTO LIQUIDI
COFANO MOTORE FISSO IN TERMOPLASTICO
BICOMPONENTE

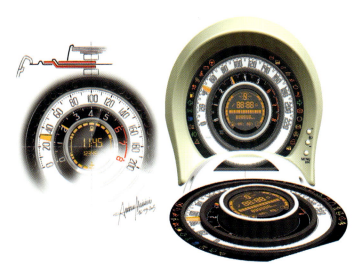

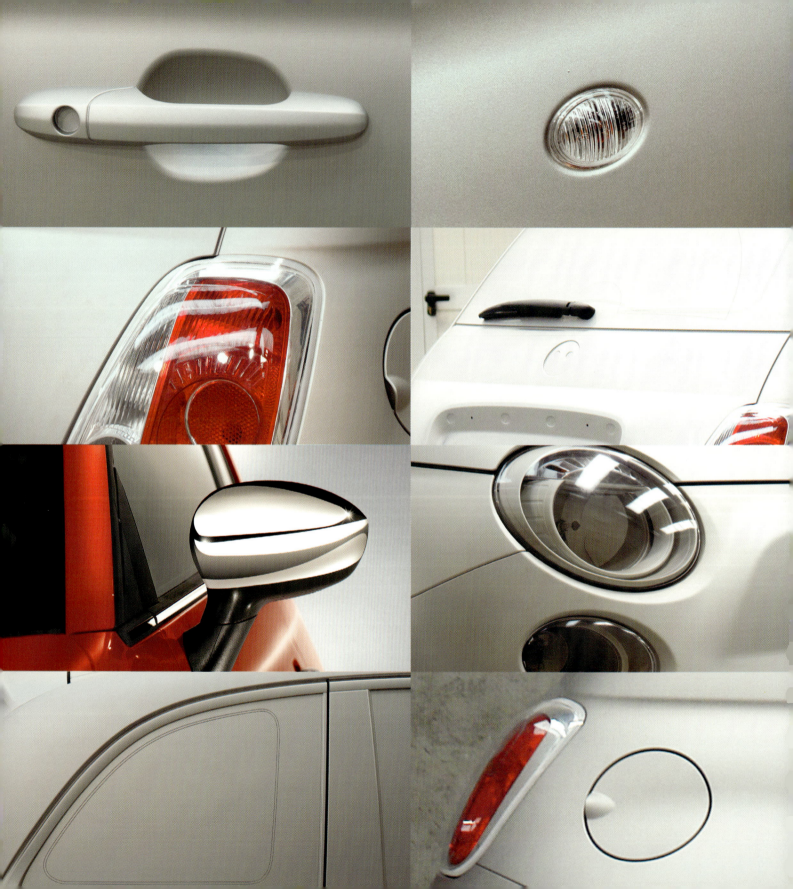

THE EVENTS OF THESE MOST RECENT YEARS HAVE HELPED US TO DISCOVER CUSTOMERS TODAY WHO ARE ATTRACTED TO AND INTERESTED IN DESIGN AS AN EMOTIONAL FACTOR, AN ELEMENT THAT BREATHES NEW LIFE INTO EVERYDAY EXPERIENCES THAT ARE BOTH POSITIVE AND GRATIFYING, ALMOST ALWAYS IN COMPLETE HARMONY WITH THE ECOLOGICAL MISSION OF THE PRODUCT THEY ARE THINKING ABOUT BUYING.

Roberto Giolito

500 WANTS YOU

What came first, the 500 or the advertising for the 500? A long way from the eternal "chicken or the egg" issue, the question reflects a new way the car itself was presented, of which the 500 has been and still is the standard-bearer. Well before knowing whether the 500 was going to look like the nice Trepiuno concept or not—the Trepiuno had broken many hearts—the advertising for the new 500 had already invaded many media channels. In particular the Internet, with the platform 500 WANTS YOU. You could configure your car, accessorize it, and redesign it. And you could interact with the Centro Stile and suggest some variations, too. Above all you could be a part of it all, leave your own mark; become a piece—however small—of a car that would definitely leave its mark on a whole era.

REVOLUTIONAIR

It wouldn't have been too difficult to draw the remake of an icon such as the 500. All that had to be done was copy the most obvious lines and the most significant details, and the public would have greeted it with open arms. But from the very start, this new 500 did not just want to be a remake. It wanted to be a real car, the perfect city car of the third millennium. The evocative and attractive design was certainly not just an "accessory." Besides the art of the stylist, there was, above all, a lot of substance: efficiency, ecology, safety, comfort, and versatility. The list of factors that define the quality of a modern vehicle is certainly not a short one. Behind every item there are great innovations and a huge amount of work in development, which doesn't end until the last car rolls off the assembly line. In 2007 the 500, with all its engines, Euro 4, was already at the cutting edge. Today the whole range features Euro 5 emission engines, with the environmental champion being the brand new two-cylinder TwinAir.

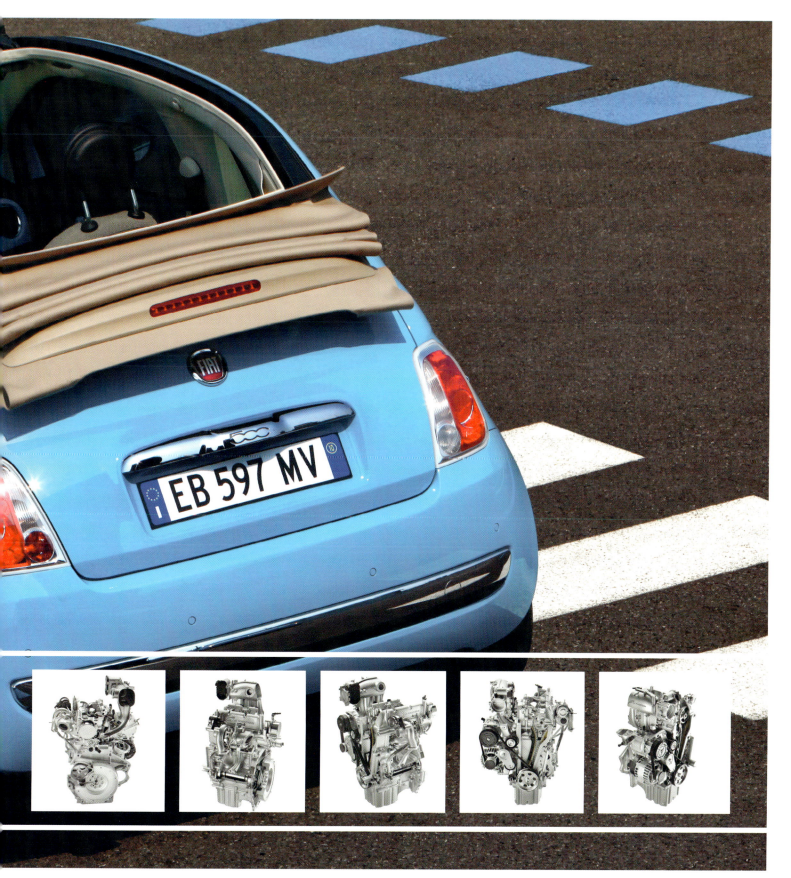

Miracolo a Milano is a temporary installation created in 2009 by Fabio Novembre on Via Montenapoleone, in Milan, as a symbol of an ecological course necessary to relaunch the image of the city.

FIVE STARS EURONCAP

Safety is a mandatory priority for the designer. There are laws, regulations, and tests to be passed. Competition gets tougher, as do the demands of a careful, well-informed public, certainly not willing to accept compromises. Not even—actually especially—when there's talk of city cars because what's reassuring on a 5-meter-long sedan or on an SUV is its size, its weight; and safety is almost always taken for granted, though sometimes mistakes are made.

When the "size" is reduced, the technology has to adjust: the study of the chassis, the ergonomics of the interiors, and all the vehicle's features. On the 500 there were seven air bags. Every single detail of a very modern platform had been carefully analyzed in order to protect the occupants, save their lives in the event of an accident, and be respectful of pedestrians.

But even more important is active safety: safe and sincere road behavior, capable of avoiding an accident. This lies in the equipment, but even more so in good design, starting from the very first line sketched on the page.

READY, STEADY, GO!

A parade of 120 cars across Turin—with 120 beauty queens on board. The presentation of the "old" 500 was probably a big event too, although the word "event" in 1957 didn't mean what it does today.

In spite of the challenging precedent, and a public by now tired of extravagant and grandiose presentations, the launch of the 500, again in July, but this time in 2007, was able to astonish, attract attention, amuse, and also not make a live television show seem somewhat presumptuous. The Winter Olympics had given new life to the city of Turin, transforming its rather gray image of a "city-factory." Exactly one year later, here were the same directorship, that of Marco Balich, and the same colorful approach that had painted Turin and Italy in Olympic colors during the opening ceremony, frescoing another face of the Bel Paese, the one that the 500 had represented in the past and that it would continue to represent in the future. Just as colorful, optimistic, and charming. Practically speaking, one and the same.

UGO NESPOLO

THE DREAM THAT MONEY CAN BUY

Perhaps it's a matter of thinking back to the historical avant-gardes, perhaps even more so to the futuristic movement that so much and so little has been said about. Of course, the ideal locus that links the world of art to the world of industry and merchandising is more or less seen as one of those ideas that aren't afraid to bring together the sacred and the profane, art and communication, and all the rest. The figure of the artist also reaffirms its connection to everyday objects, to technological innovations, and he feels lucky whenever he can combine them in his own work, his own vision, even in his own "style," in the same way that some of the greatest artists from the past—from de Chirico to Depero, Balla, Prampolini, and all the others—were willing to do. The 500 is truly a legendary object. The object of our earliest youth—a democratic and loyal companion—this new miracle of technology and design is ready to let us once again dream a possible dream. With great pleasure I have tried to communicate the widespread energy, joyfulness, even the good taste that surrounds this tiny miracle.
It didn't seem like such a hard thing to do!
Have I been able to?

20%
ROMANCE

20%
PASSION

20%
FUN

20%
FREEDOM

20%
CREATIVITY

20%
COMMUNICATION

20%
STYLE

20%
PERSONALITY

20%
GLAMOUR

20%
OPTIMISM

ON THE ROAD

3

A CINQUECENTO IN MANHATTAN

Evolution without revolution.
The 500 is all grown up and
ready to cross new frontiers.

GREAT, WHAT IS IT? THERE IT SITS—A ROUND WHITE THING ON THE ASPHALT OF PARK AVENUE, LIKE A SCOOP OF VANILLA ICE CREAM FALLEN OUT OF THE HANDS OF A LARGE AND CLUMSY CONCRETE CHILD.

VITTORIO ZUCCONI

I'm afraid it might melt under my behind, or that one of the skyscrapers around me will bend over like in a Disney cartoon to pick up off the sidewalk, while scolding the child, the first Fiat 500 ever seen in New York City. The doorman at the Waldorf Astoria, with his decorative braidings, collar badges, and admiral's cap, trained to park limousines that are necessarily black, possibly a hundred yards long, looks with astonishment at my scoop of ice cream as it slips in between the aircraft-carrier-sized funeral hearses that hes used to maneuvering. He seems undecided as to whether to kick me out with a broom the way he would young hoods in an alleyway or to search for a hook so he can load it onto the porters trolley and have it sent up to my room. Only a green twenty-dollar bill, which at the Waldorf is like the fifty cents for a windshield washer in Rome, softens him up, at least until two people on bicycles stop between the limousines to ask what that little white thing they've never seen before is. "It's your next bicycle, but less tiring," I reply, which offends them and the doorman at the same time.

Now I know what Tom Thumb must have felt like while tangling with giants. Challenging the brashest city in the world from behind the steering wheel of the shyest and tiniest car in the world is the perfect metaphor for the "crazy flight" that Fiat now Chrysler, or Chrysler now Fiat, has decided to launch in the America of towering heights and endless distances, where thousands of miles on the highway are a mere out-of-town trip and 5-liter seven-seaters are compact family cars. And yet if this scoop of metallic white ice cream has any hope of making it anywhere it's here, among the Cyclops of Park Avenue, in Chinatown's alleyways, in the self-referential aloofness of the Village, in the metropolitan canyons of Fifth Avenue, in this universe that gave us Seinfeld, Woody Allen, and *Sex and the City*; where it just might arouse the spoiled imagination of the city's young princes and princesses. The first human test, not the kind that terrorizes the engineers and the designers, must therefore inevitably be the "magnet test," i.e., "Sex and the Cinquecento."

On the eastern shore of the East River, in the shadow of the bridge that stretches from Brooklyn all the way to the island of Manhattan, a gigantic 1957 Buick, the exact opposite of my white scoop with its wide-open eyes, comes barreling my way out of the blue, still triumphantly armed with its tail fins, chrome trim, and warlike fenders. It gets sucked up by my Thumbelina and a lady steps out, more or less the same age as the first 500 launched in 1957, although she does her best, with a miniskirt and makeup, to fool Chronos, the god of time. "What a darling, how cute," she says as she rubs what's left of her curves around the solid ones on my metallic dumpling that luckily for her are without spurs or fins, and also tells me that she too is Italian in a language that is still comprehensible. "Hello, darling [this time I'm the darling in question, so it's flirting between peers now], *mi chiamo Ginetta Vendetta* [right!]." Then she whispers to me, purring, "And I'm a really good trumpet player." To avoid a misunderstanding, from out of Ginetta Vendetta's bosom comes a business card adorned with musical notes and tiny trumpets. The magnet on wheels has done its job, even if, as with all magnets, you never know which iron scrap or filings it'll pick up.

The anxiety creeps up again on the Brooklyn Bridge, as I—so to speak—race toward the Cyclops rising up on the island surrounded by the plays of light on the water. In front of the cafés and bistros and restaurants with their fusion cuisine (mix once, mix twice, something or the other will emerge from the kitchen) females of a more recent generation crowd around my 500, whimpering with desire. Although they're not exactly the kind that buys Manolo Blahnik shoes, they are promising—for the car, not for the driver, let's be clear. "I *want* one of these now, can you give me one?" a pair of high heels, stilettos they call them here, implores. Unfortunately it's not mine. "Look, it even has a trunk for shopping," a lady who's just come out of the Fiat Café at the Bowery, on Mott Street, enthuses—needless to say, hanging on the walls are photos of all the versions of this baby's forefather and at least fifty die-cast models of the same. "Ah, oui," the café owner joins in with the tweeting of the young girls, "*Elle est mignonne cette petite*," he judges, pretty, small. Would you buy one? Never. Ah, well then. "But I'll definitely put a picture of it up on the wall right away." He stands still and takes the picture. Better than nothing, Mr. Marchionne. "But where's the engine?" an elderly passerby asks, who swears he paid tribute to Fiat some forty years ago. Up front. He seems a little disappointed. Lou, the owner, comes out of the Di Palo *groceria*, the last real Italian delicatessen in Little Italy that's by now turned into part of Chinatown. "Nice. Fiat?" Fiat. "The last time I was in Italy I hired a van—that's right, a Fiat van, and it left me stuck on the highway like a jerk." Might be some bias here.

When the huge truck had unloaded it in front of me, under the gaze of the New York police force—whose level of interest moved them to overlook the fact that it had no plates apart from the temporary one from Detroit, Michigan, and an almost invisible one in the rear window—more than the Manhattan cops, there were two things I was afraid of: the yellow cabs, the ones that move like packs of sharks driven by kamikaze pilots who failed their driving test in Kabul, and the holes, those potholes that swallow up cars whole, leaving no trace behind, or that, hastily covered over with steel sheets and so uneven they look like makeshift tiers at a stadium, deform tires and crush suspensions. (Relax, Mr. Marchionne: not even a fine, not even a scratch, and even the six-speed gear box, uselessly mandatory now in all cars, clicked into action like a Swiss army knife, dispelling my youthful memories of nonsynchronized transmission.) But Tom Thumb, who still doesn't like highways, accustomed as he is to living in the urban jungle with his younger brothers, doesn't cry, doesn't creak, doesn't bend out of shape. He sinks and emerges all in one piece, ready to take on the next ogre, like horses wading across the fords of the Wild West. The risk is actually the traffic light at the corner of Fifth and Fifty-Seventh, in front of Van Cleef & Arpels—the favorite jeweler of Jackie Onassis, where the humblest of trinkets costs twice as much as my ice cream—and human walls surround me in the nonstop transhumance of a delightful weekend of fall shopping. Behind the wheel, at the height of their handbags and shopping bags, I feel like the cat with a long tail in a discothèque, but the people, even the feral tourist in Manhattan, even the tall guy who hoped in vain to make it in professional basketball, whose knees I come up to, move around my 500 with the tenderness of relatives in the newborn nursery, bending over three times just to talk to me. "Cool car." I can hear their voices echo, "This car is awesome," "I love Fiat" (I wasn't expecting this one at all). "I had a Fiat 128 once," a passerby well past middle age says as he smiles at me, and I find the fact that he smiles at me, now that he's made me remember that 1970s disaster, says a great deal about human forgiveness. Leaning up against a traffic light, a stupendous member of the female gender—at least I think she is—her legs twice as long and her age half as old as my trumpet-playing Ginetta, tries to ignore me; the car, I mean.

She looks up, sighs with boredom, but then gives in and gives me a smile worthy of a Park Avenue orthodontist. She does so with perfect timing, with the craftiness of only the very beautiful and only the very used to this sort of thing, as soon as the Red Sea of the crowd around me parts and the green light forces me to unleash the eager Polish ponies designed in Turin and to gallop away. But it works, it works. I mean, the car, of course.

After a lengthy and articulate debate with the tourist bus driver, in front of the inevitable Apollo Theater in Harlem ("The engine seems good, looks comfortable inside," he concludes, he, who with a wag of his tail on the highway, with his bus that has satellite TV, a toilet, eight gears, and a self-governed diesel engine that could send me flying off to another state like a baseball), will be the final test of love, passed with flying colors, in the evening, in front of one of the most popular Italian restaurants of the moment. In the October darkness that by now falls fast, in between the private German bullies and the stretch limos of the exhibitionists, in front of the sumptuous Del Posto, one of the dozen or so in the gastronomic empire created by the indefatigable Dalmatian refugee Lidia Bastianich (now also opened in Singapore), the doorman unsheathes orange parking cones to make room for the scoop of ice cream, under the annoyed gaze of the Indians, meaning the sons of the Asian subcontinent, who seem to have monopolized the limousine business in New York. "What the fuck is it?" a driver dares to ask vulgarly, and is immediately punished by Tom Thumb's protectors, who force his "serious" car to go around the block once more before letting his clients off. It's obvious that he sees my little scoop as an enemy, a lethal competitor, and realizes the possibility that the 500, with no hope of conquering the great distances of the Midwest and the Prairie, will steal his customers in the urban chaos of Los Angeles, Chicago, New York, and Miami.

The empress of catering comes out too, Lidia, who touches it and lets herself be photographed beside it. I shamelessly park it in front of the restaurant, breaking all the rules and codes, a tiny weary Gulliver, but victorious after a Saturday of war in Manhattan defended by an army of orange Lilliputians. I leave it open, the windows lowered, tender and vulnerable. "But aren't you afraid they'll steal it?" Gabriele, the photographer, asks me. "No, I'm not, Gabriele. If anything, I'm afraid they'll eat it up."

Vittorio Zucconi

More than fifty years had gone by and everything seemed different somehow: the lights, the colors, the fashions. Even the skyline was different. Some skyscrapers now rocketed skyward while others had disappeared, bearing witness to the passing of time or—in some cases—great historical events that marked an era.

AND THEN THERE WERE SOME "THINGS" THAT NEVER CHANGE, WHETHER THEY'RE SPECIAL ATMOSPHERES, THE FEATURES OF A CERTAIN STYLE, OR EMOTIONS. NEW YORK WILL ALWAYS BE THE BIG APPLE AND THE 500 WILL ALWAYS BE THE 500, EVEN FIFTY YEARS LATER.

THE CONQUEST OF AMERICA

"IT'S GOING TO BE A THRILL TO SEE THE 500 IN ACTION, AND NOT JUST ON THE STREETS OF AMERICAN CITIES, BUT ON THE GRIDLOCKED HIGHWAYS TOO, WHERE OFTEN THE SPEED LIMIT IS NOT MORE THAN 30 MILES AN HOUR AND THE USE OF HUGE SUVS JUST TO GET TO THE OFFICE IS HARD TO JUSTIFY."

With these words Roberto Giolito, a sort of "father" to the new 500, anticipated the moment of the car's landing on the North American market. The year 2009 was coming to an end. The agreement between Fiat and Chrysler was much more than just something in the air, and the elements that would become the strong points and the marketing strategies of the "American" 500 were already starting to transpire: emotion, functionality, style, ecology, and expressiveness—concepts we'd be hearing a lot about.

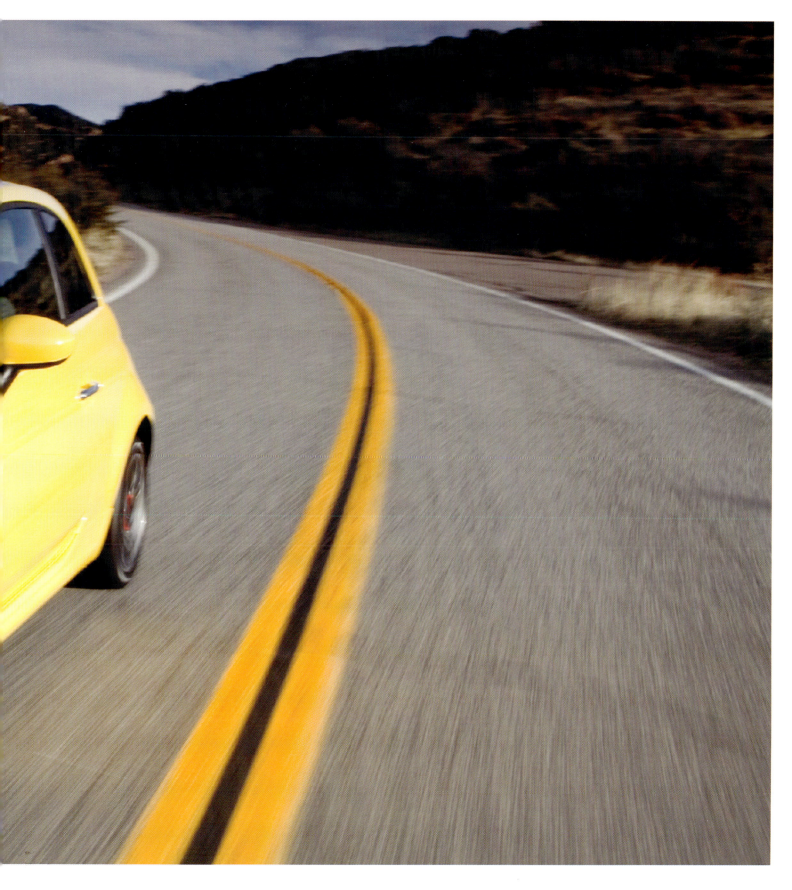

HOW MUCH ITALY IS THERE IN THE 500? MAYBE NOT THE ITALY OF PIZZA, AND MAYBE NOT EVEN THAT OF MUSIC—WHETHER CLASSICAL, EASY LISTENING, OR POP—BUT THERE IS DEFINITELY THE ITALY THAT DEDICATES TIME TO COOK AND SAVOR ITS FOOD OR A SONG.

The enthusiasm for life comes about through love and attention to detail. The excitement, the happiness one feels for the little things, and the ability to appreciate beauty. It means being in love with the life that has produced the great masterpieces of art and that today encourages people to seek the artistic and creative sides in every object—where design is no longer simply an accessory at the service of function, but a genuine need.

PASSION
A passion for life, beauty, nature.
Young and youthful passion.

SIMPLICITY & MODERNITY
No compromising, no facades:
a love for the pure and simple life.

COMMUNICATION

Communication means that there's never any passiveness. It means sincere relationships—active, fresh, and fast.

INDIVIDUAL EXPRESSION

The car as a point of view and representation. Customized and modeled to fit the user's personality.

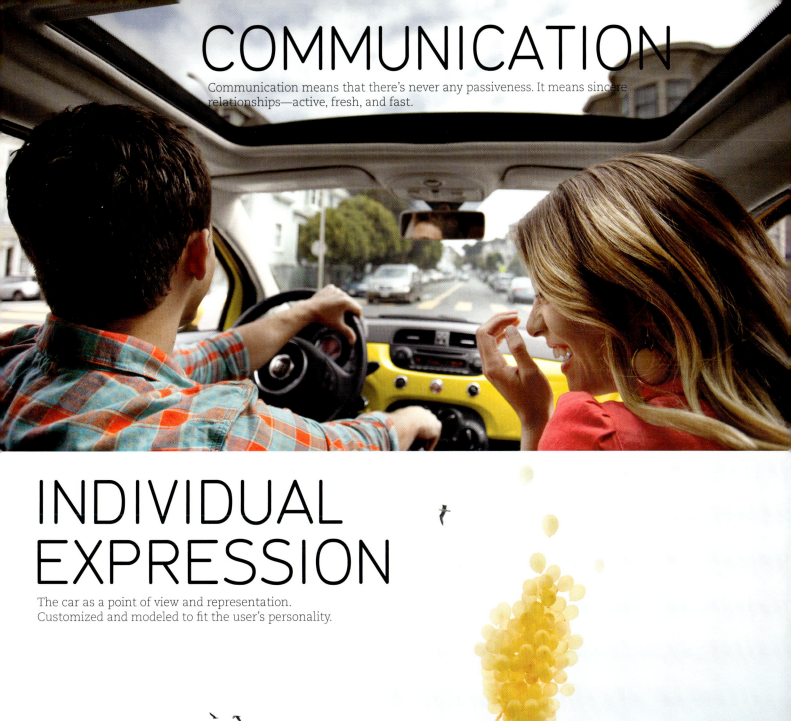

YOU HAVE TO ZERO IN
AND USE A MEASURING
TAPE TO COMPARE
THE TWO 500s
IN ORDER TO SEE THAT
THE "AMERICAN" 500
IS ALMOST COMPLETELY
NEW AS COMPARED TO
ITS COUSIN FROM THE
OLD WORLD.

ON OUR WAY TO THE USA

At first sight it really looks a lot like her. It has that same inviting expression on its "face." And if we look a little closer we can really only see a few differences. You have to zero in and use a measuring tape to compare the two 500s in order to see that the "American" 500 is almost completely new as compared to its cousin from the Old World.

In describing the newest-born we often fall into the trap of highlighting the innovations as compared to the European version. But it's not just a "game" of finding the differences because the "starting point" is a car that has earned more than sixty international awards—including Car of the Year in 2008—and that has managed to win over more than five hundred thousand customers in three years. The comparison is therefore a way to applaud the great work that technicians and designers have put into designing a car that represents absolute excellence.

The proof of this will be in the 2012 version, when many of the improvements introduced to the U.S. version—judged by the press to be the best of the 500s—will also be seen in the European models.

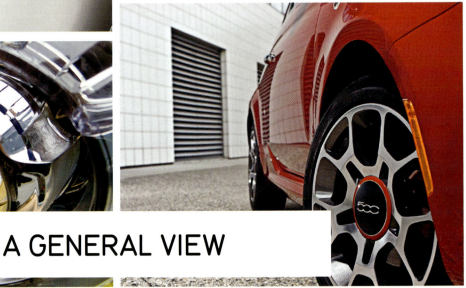

A GENERAL VIEW

IN MANY CASES IT'S A QUESTION OF REGULATIONS, WHICH DIFFER GREATLY BETWEEN EUROPE AND THE UNITED STATES: LIGHTS WITH A DIFFERENT SHAPE, TECHNOLOGY AND SIZE, SIDE-MARKERS, THE SHAPE OF THE REGISTRATION PLATE HOLDER, FENDERS CAPABLE OF PASSING CRASH TESTS—AND MUCH MORE.

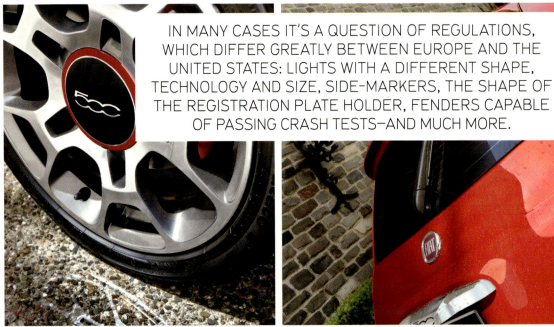

At times the demands are dictated by the climate, by the customers' tastes, and by practical needs. They might be considered just details, such as the alloy rims with a protective edge that won't get scratched at the automatic car wash. But the details are what make the difference.

What one notices right away is the introduction of a new body for the Sports version: the fenders—front and rear—have a sporty design, with large three-part, aggressive openings . . . as we wait for the 500 Abarth!

BEHIND THE WHEEL

THE INSIDE IS THE SAME AS THE OUTSIDE: EVERYTHING IS COMPLETELY NEW, AND AT THE SAME TIME EVERYTHING IS UNMISTAKABLY 500.

What we find now are those indispensable cup-holders and more comfortable seats, for trips that will probably be longer. There are different materials, finishings, details, and colors, on which a more careful assembly of the central dashboard stands out.

But it's when we sit behind the steering wheel that we notice the real turnabout; the soundproofing has been completely done over, with the adoption of sound-absorbent materials on the body, and the equipping of the engine with supports and covers capable of dampening the vibrations and the noise. Even the air-conditioning is specific, capable of guaranteeing the maximum comfort in extreme climates, from the glaciers of Canada to the intense heat of the equatorial zones.

THE MECHANICS BEHIND THE DREAM

The rear of the car is hit perpendicularly by a trolley weighing 1,100 kg and moving at a speed of 36 kph: this is the norm that governs one of the European crash tests meant to test the resilience of the fuel tank. In America the trolley weighs 1,368 kg and moves at a speed of 80 kph. And after the impact, the car is lifted and turned over to check for any leaks.

This is only one of the many possible examples to explain just how different the rules are between the two continents and, consequently, how much the engineering of the 500 has had to be updated: enhanced front and rear transverse crossbars, strengthened sides, differently shaped air bags and also revised suspensions, a quieter braking system, and an Aisin six-speed automatic transmission to satisfy the customers' tastes traditionally not inclined to using a clutch. Although, because it is an Italian car, it's also available with a manual gearshift.

Lastly, under the hood is one of the key points of the Fiat-Chrysler agreement, signed in 2009 with the "blessings" of the U.S. government: an engine with MultiAir technology. From a technical standpoint—very briefly—it's a system that, owing to an electrohydraulic device controlled from the electronic circuit board, allows optimum intake valve opening schedules. Practically speaking, there's a 10 percent power hike (currently, the aspirated 1.4 cc features 102 bhp) together with a decrease in consumption and, above all, in polluting emissions.

That typically (even if not exclusively) Italian phenomenon that was the 500 in 1957 was produced in the very Italian Turin, at the Mirafiori plant. The "new" 500 was born during the time of globalization and—at least in the Old World—distances were shrinking, so much so that the model plant of Tichy, in Poland, seemed to be just around the corner. The definitive turnaround, instead, sees the crossing of the Atlantic, and the equipping of the plant in Toluca, Mexico, where the 500s destined for the United States—and also for the South American countries starting in Brazil—are assembled.

The 500 of 2012 is not merely a question of geographic distance. What American drivers will be presented with is a completely new car, one that was born in America and designed for this market—so different from that in Europe. And on these roads, in the test centers of the Chrysler Group, the new 500 will have done more than four million miles: different latitudes, climates, surfaces, and conditions, for a long and meticulous work of fine-tuning. A painstaking job that customers are unaware of, but that they can appreciate in their everyday use of the car.

Once again, with a new generation, the inside parts change, even the leather. But the distinctive soul of the 500 has not changed one bit.

TOLUCA MEXICO **2011**

THE EVOLUTION OF THE SPECIES

IN THE UNITED STATES, THE 500 DEBUTED WITH A LIMITED SERIES OF CARS CALLED "PRIMA EDIZIONE," WRITTEN JUST LIKE THAT, IN ITALIAN. AND THE SAME THING HAPPENED IN ITALY WITH THE "OPENING EDITION," BUT THIS TIME WRITTEN IN ENGLISH. THERE ARE THREE VERSIONS TO CHOOSE FROM: POP, THE ENTRY LEVEL, AND THE TWO SPORT AND LOUNGE VERSIONS, OFFERED AS ALTERNATIVES FOR MORE AMBITIOUS CUSTOMERS. RICHER, MORE COMPLETE, AND MORE SOPHISTICATED ACCESSORIES ARE WHAT EMPHASIZE THE CAR'S SPORTINESS AND ELEGANCE, RESPECTIVELY, BUT ALWAYS IN A YOUTHFUL AND TRENDY WAY. THE OPTION TO CUSTOMIZE THE CAR IS BROAD, FROM THE COLORS OF THE BODY ALL THE WAY DOWN TO THE TINIEST DETAILS, AND AS TIME GOES BY, THANKS TO THE LAUNCH OF NEW MODELS, THERE WILL BE MORE AND MORE ALTERNATIVES. BUT THIS IS JUST THE BEGINNING: THE 500C IS RIGHT BEHIND IT, AND ALREADY THERE'S TALK OF THE "MEAN" VERSION WITH THE SCORPION, THE ONE FROM THE ABARTH, ON THE HOOD. BUT THE IDEA OF AN ELECTRIC 500 IS STILL TOP SECRET.

LIFE IS BEST
WHEN DRIVEN BY...
LIFE ISN'T BEST WHEN DRIVEN BY ONE THING. LIFE IS BEST WHEN DRIVEN BY LOTS OF THINGS. DEPENDING ON HOW FAR YOU WANT TO GO, THE FIAT 500 WILL TAKE YOU THERE.

In American cities you can literally see them everywhere, with New York being the first place. The billboards in the series that reads: "Life is best when driven by . . ." are much more than advertising; they are the declaration of intent of a car that doesn't want to go by unnoticed and that doesn't want to become one of the many, anonymous items in the price lists inside car magazines that are almost always read, analyzed, and scrutinized more with a rational eye than an emotional one. 500 is the state of the art in its segment and its times, but it also wants you to fall in love with it.

BY PASSION. BY NECESSITY.
BY CURIOSITY. BY STYLE. BY DESIRE.
BY INHIBITION. BY WILL. BY VISION.
BY VIGOR. BY IMPULSE. BY LONGING.
BY FORCE. BY EUPHORIA. BY ANGST.
BY ECSTASY. BY THIRST. BY WHIMSY.
BY LUST. BY FERVOR. BY AWE.
BY HUNGER. BY INFATUATION.
BY WONDER. BY THRILL. BY RAPTURE.
BY CURIOSITY. BY ARDOR. BY DEFIANCE.
BY PLEASURE. BY FANTASY. BY ZEAL . . .

PHOTOGRAPHY CREDITS

Archivio Storico Fiat: 10–11, 16–17, 18–19, 20–21, 22–23, 24–25, 26, 27 (background image), 28–29, 30, 31, 34, 35, 36, 37, 40, 41, 42, 43, 44, 45, 46–47, 48, 49, 50, 52-53, 60, 61, 62, 63, 64, 65, 66, 67, 76–77, 110 (foreground and background images)

Centro Stile Fiat: 6–7, 82, 83, 84, 85, 86, 87, 88, 89, 90–91

www.fiatgroupautomobilespress.com: 32–33, 38–39, 54–55, 70–71, 72, 74–75, 78-79, 80, 81, 88 (detail images in color), 89 (detail images in color), 92–93, 94, 95, 96–97, 98–99, 102–103, 120–121, 129 (smaller image)

Chrysler Group LLC: 12–13, 104–105, 111, 112–113, 114–115, 116–117, 118, 119, 123, 124–125, 126, 127, 128, 129, 130–131, 132, 134–135, 136–137, 138–139, 142–143

Courtesy Ron Arad: 58
Courtesy Roberto Acotto: 22 (Fiat 500 Giannini)
Courtesy Romeo Ferraris: 77 (Fiat 500 Monza Romeo Ferraris)
Courtesy Carrozzeria Castagna Milano: 77 (Fiat 500 Tender Two Castagna)

© Ugo Nespolo: 100, 101

Every effort has been made to credit the copyright holders of the images used in this book. Any inaccuracies or omissions brought to the publisher's attention will be corrected in future editions.